Night Ribbons

Cynthia Gallaher

D0916073

Polar Bear Press, Chicago

Acknowledgements
Works listed have first appeared in the following:
"An Old Habit of Mine", "Geisha House" and "Trespass-
ers", *Korone*: An Anthology of Illinois Women Writers,
1987; "Portrait of a Woman", *Imagine*: An International
Journal of Chicano Literature(Feminist Issue), 1985; "Self-
Portrait in a Game of Pool" and "Bellydancer", *Lucky Star*,
Erie Street Press, 1984-86; "Dream Before the Earth-
quake", *Emergency Tacos* anthology, 1989; "El Dia de los
Muertos", *California Quarterly*, 1986; "The Invisible",
Pikestaff Forum, 1987; "Man Learned to Dance Before He
Could Walk", *Oyez Review*, 1986; "Paris Windows", *Black
& White*, 1987; "And Lead Him Not Into Penn Station",
Scrap Paper Review, 1988; "Black & White: A Zebra's
View", *Zoo Poems* anthology, 1988.

ISBN#0-9623803-0-X

Library of Congress Card Catalog Number: 89-92373

This project is partially supported by a grant from the
Department of Cultural Affairs, Office of Fine Arts, and
the Illinois Arts Council Access Program.

For additional copies, order from:
Polar Bear Press
PO Box A3604
Chicago, Illinois 60690

For Carlos

Table of Contents

Women of Day and Night
An Old Habit of Mine/7
Salmon/9
Cavallo/11
Portrait of a Woman/15
Geisha House/16
Trespassers/18
Bellydancer/20
See Rock City/22

Chicago Days and Nights
Popping Tar Bubbles/25
The Man Who
Taught Me to Swim/27
Darkroom/28
Shabbona Park District
Swimming Pool/29
The Building That
Does Not Dance/31
Self-Portrait in a
Game of Pool/34
The Squash Garden/35

Donde Hablan Español
Dream Before the Earthquake/37
El Dia de los Muertos/38
The Invisible/39
On the Other Side/41
The Last Father/42

Ancient Days, Far Away Nights
Man Learned to Dance
Before He Could Walk/44
Lucifer, The Morning Star/47
Paris Windows/49
The Wheel/51
The Fourth Fiber/54
Quarter American/56
The Writing's on the Wall/57
And Lead Him Not
Into Penn Station/58
Black and White:
A Zebra's View/62

An Old Habit of Mine

Mirror, chest, and slim bed,
    a room as anyone's room,
like one in a minor hotel,
but here the Bible lies open,
not tucked in a nightstand
    like an oversized sachet.
No dustballs in the corners
    belie my sloth,
or is there clutter,
    even on covered shelves.
One candle, however, burns with a
wild raggedness
after I close my door.

For a life devoted to prayer,
there are plenty of times
my fervency spills into
    sun-drenched scenarios,
complete with well-oiled
    former boyfriends,
but as in the fairytale
where the girl fell down a well
    and discovered a secret kingdom,
the major part of me's
    gone underground,
where union with the Spirit
has pierced deeper
than the warmest body.

I tell my catechism students
there's a punk hairdo
    under my veil -
cut with a machete
    when on mission
        in Central America.

My superiors remind me this type
    of humor is
reserved for priests,
as is the chalice that
    becomes blood
    at each mass.
I continue to flow
month in,
month out,
and remain childless
    as Jesus.
My former life is as colorful
    as hopscotch pastels,
    as stained as
    crushed cigarettes,
until rain thundered
on the walks.
Now I move barefoot in my shoes,
am naked, when covered.

Salmon

I wear jogging shoes at night
to leap into cabs quickly
   if I have to,
   and you can see the shimmer
   of my dress only
if you come up close.
A dozen different men call me Maureen,
the code name around Grand Central Station,
but I heard it once or twice
   last night
as I worked my way around
42nd and 8th.
As soon as the cops get wind of it,
the name will change as quickly
as directions of those Hurricanes
off the Atlantic coast,
that all-girl gang I ran with
in my younger days.

For every fish that tugged
the nets of my daddy's boat
there is a man that tugs
   my stockings as if they were
   veils to pillars of wisdom,
or the sirens that called to
   Odysseus from cliffs
   of the Aegean Sea.
My hips move steady
in the hands of oarsmen
landlocked in the 20th Century,
they call me mermaid, water baby,
   Veronica Lake,
their mooring — marina —
Maureen.

They take their hooks out
and watch me slip
   through their fingers
and dive back between traffic
   that turns like water
   in a flume
at the West Terminal.

Every once in a while
I long for a warm place,
with cases lined in shells,
deep laughter from the kitchen,
amd sounds of splashing water
from the bathtub,
But if I fought my way up river,
   it would only take me to New Jersey,
and my ability to spawn was cut short
   years ago
   in three flashes of silver
   at the doctor's office,
But most of all, the only men I really know
   are neither fishermen, boatswags nor
   explorers of the seven seas,
but merely stuntmen in barrels,
tumbling over falls for a few brief moments,
before drifting back in darkness to
   Des Moines, Indianapolis,
            Cincinnati.

Cavallo

Cavallo, it was you
who sat in front of me
in third grade.
I remember your hair like wire,
(I always studied the
back of your head),
your hips full, and thighs like
loaves of bread cradled
on a wooden dish
carved by students
before you.

Your form and others
in the room
appeared the September after
they pried city blocks
of your kind from homes
on Taylor Street,
replacing nearly every Italian member
of Chicago's extended family
with studies on the disappearance
of the same,
Masters' programs conducted
in phantoms of your kitchens.

There was little glamorous
in your attached housing
behind the school,
but the smell of garlic
from your window
made rooms seem sensual
enormous,
laughter reached outside
like a bird's flight
to the highest branch,
gone, the smell of boiled potatoes,

the dry starch of pleated curtains
of the Swedes and Germans
who'd gone on to conquer
Schaumburg and Hoffman Estates.

Your mother never
let us inside,
embarrassed by the worn furniture,
and your dad would travel
up one block, down the next,
like a peddler,
but with pretense of walking the dog.
He, too, seemed on a leash,
one the city had tied to a post
　in the concrete stamp
　they called your backyard,
letting him run a few blocks
　to the bright lights of
the intersection,
yet always pulling him back by the neck
to those rented quarters
that were never really yours.

Cavallo, you were first
to become woman in our class,
first with bra and the
hesitant start of a monthly flow,
and like an oracle,
you spoke to us
from the other side,
of what was to come.

In high school, you slimmed down,
shared secrets behind cupped hands,
jokes out loud in study hall.

And when fans overhead creaked
loudest on hot afternoons,
you pined most for Italian lemonade
under huge green and red umbrellas,
and couldn't wait to start working.

I went on to the campus
you'd given your home
to accommodate.
And walking over concrete pylons and slabs
that formed a shell
where your house once stood,
I thought of your beginnings,
that former layer,
an exiled civilization.

Years tallied, and rumor
had it you ran off,
eloped with with a
soldier in Germany.
You couldn't quite make it
back to your homeland,
but could pin down and question
German architects
who inspired granite walls
that replaced your three flats.

You had a little boy for awhile,
not really German, Italian, or American,
and death, also without nationality,
and loyal to no one,
wrestled the child from your arms,
shook you from a marriage riddled in blame,
and found you back in America,
an immigrant again, a refugee.

Standing in the playlot
we knew as kids,
you release the spirit of your boy
to ghosts of your ancestors,
    who sing Italian songs
    late at night
    from a porch you've never seen.
On the family screen door now,
A large "C" appears in cast iron,
an attempt at a new tradition,
you knock,
your widowed mother,
apprehensive at the door,
even of you.

Portrait of A Woman

Bundled in furs,
walking down 5th Avenue,
it's the afternoon custom.
The winter wind's sharp teeth
   are just about to nip her heels -
narrow, sculptured, covered in kidskin,
she sidesteps
   through revolving doors,
hours pass in fitting rooms,
   in other people's clothes,
sparkling ensembles grow heavy as she
   looks into full-length mirrors
   accustomed to dozens of images
   just like herself,
in need of accessories.

The sun's angle throws its crooked eye
   between blocks of buildings,
catches her offguard as she
crosses against the light.
She stands
for one frantic moment,
awake for the first time in years,
   here,
on a city street corner,
the wind cutting open her coat,
the sunlight cast sharply from her earrings,
not knowing which way is home.

Geisha House

The men at the geisha houses
have changed. There are
less of the younger ones than before.
They take sex tour vacations
to Manila or request tall, blonde
demonstrators for their stateside booths
at the Consumer Electronics Show.

In the old days, sex was layered,
    rich, and intricate as the
    tightly-woven folds of
    our kimonos.
During music hour, the chords
struck on lute
symbolized the force
each client was born with.
Our pale hands and throats
were the blossom landscape
of a distant province,
far from their day tables cluttered
with abacus, glyphs, and coarse twine.

After being fed and their
feet washed in candlelight -
    the night walk home,
    with passion,
would anticipate their wives
who'd performed the same ritual
with the children -
    music, art, bath, and bed,
and how like a prowling cat,
the world, for a few hours,
opened to them,
not nearly ordinary as the
lives they'd created.

Their wives, like most women
    around the world,
hard-working, with little pay
and without property,
would entertain themselves in
houses of the interior,
    the imagination,
before greeting their men, with
    hair untwined, at the door.

My daughter studies computer now.
One client of ten years' wife
    has passed away.
He visits me at home after I
    remove my makeup,
    and you can see fine lines
    around my eyes.
I serve him rice and seaweed,
which odors permeate mats
    and screens of my apartment,
but even he is beginning to smell
    of the steaks and
    sugary things of the West.
Like an artist who has sold
    every scroll to make a living,
    and given all his paintbrushes
    to his students,
I still remain true to my art,
    with kimonos folded away
    in 500 years of history,
and an audience rushing
    to embrace
a more easily-wrapped memory.

Trespassers

Why the Indians didn't pick us
to kindling wood
when we first settled
in the shadow of
  Beartooth Mountain,
baffles me.
They're without fear,
or so I read their faces
  when our wagon nears their camp,
though my husband takes
their silence
for respect.

A Blackfeet squaw gave me three
  strands of beads as milky
  and smooth as melting ice,
for an iron pot I brought
  from Minnesota,
and told of seven children
  and a husband plucked
  from the back
  of an apaloosa
by an army issue rifle.

If they saw
the many skins
which line our walls,
I think they would want
to skin us, too,
and only our kind
leaves flayed carcasses
warm on the
frozen prairie.
Still, they keep their distance.

Perhaps it's the smoke that rises
from the new fort
on the other side of the mountain,
that reminds them of
their cousins' burning villages,
where smallpox was distributed
through donated blankets,
before railroads drove spikes
through their hunting grounds.

Bellydancer

Your thighs, uncovered,
shiver as if sprayed
   with cold water,
manipulated from behind
   by someone very strong,
   invisible,
   in love with you.
Pressing warm fingers
   along the nerves
   of your spine,
making your arms move to the music.

You go into a trance, on cue,
I question it as technique,
the colored silk scarves
   of your costume,
appear from the black velvet sleeve
   of the night club's curtain,
   as a trick.
Tables of Greek men in the audience
miss it.
   So sure of themselves all week,
   in their bakeries, real estate offices,
   or grating cabbage in their restaurants,
something escapes through pores
   on the backs of their necks,
turns them
   into objects of small game,
caught,
with a net thrown over them.

Large amber gems
   shift at your hips,
heavy with howling rhythms
   of Afghanistan,

your eyes shift like a jackal's.
You later admit hearing a
        multitude of spirit creatures,
moving like morphine in a vein,
even through cheap electronic speakers,
you can hear the terror approaching.
It seems nothing can restrain you,
music wails up and down
        like waves of blood,
a voice flat as a desert
        reaches out like a
        desperate animal,
by now, you're completely hidden
        by layers of filmy cloth
        as you spin,
only a heart woven
        heavily and intricately
        as a rug could reach you.

It reaches you,
after a night of wrestling
        with an audience,
        with the illusions
        you've trained your body
        to convey as revelation,
a message reaches you by dawn,
as your hand holds, not finger cymbals,
        but a camel-hair brush,
        water painting Annunciations.

See Rock City

Once off the elevator,
they enter the cave's theater,
and like an usher,
I cradle a flashlight
in hands draped
in the whitest gloves.
Along edges of non-slip shoes,
I've attached reflector tape
so the tour group follows every step.
One glove pulls a huge handle
igniting a row of lights,
coral pinks and jamaican blues
bathing 32-inch stalagtites.
The group sighs in unison.
Newlyweds study these icy, pastel tongues
and allow their own hands
to turn hot and molten as young steel.
From behind hidden speakers,
a cassette tape hesitates,
then blares the cave's cold history
with its network of channels,
whose silence is consumed by
a wrathful voice.
A blond woman fingers pearls,
stares at a pool of blind fish,
tosses a coin
in their midst.
An elderly man lags behind,
a trick he learned in the war.
He examines rocks closely
to confirm they're not merely
papier-mache over chicken wire.
I study faces before me,
they seem to harden into expressions
of wax, lost, distracted.

We trek our way back
to the souvenir shop and
ten-stool café,
where scratches of pens
on backs of postcards
replace dripping water on stone far below.

The tour guide is always the last to leave.
But instead of rinsing the coffee pot,
restocking postcards,
getting in my blue Ford and
heading home to an evening
of magazines and talkshows,
I lock myself inside,
spy the pearl-lady's fur
left behind on the coat rack.
Her oversight,
like a fleeing animal that's
snagged its pelt on a bush.

The blue blazer with gold buttons,
charcoal skirt, starched blouse,
lace panties and bra,
the standard 14-carat gold
that flashes from angles
of my body,
the glowing shoes, the flashlight
and gloves,
all come off and
find their way to the floor
of the shaft elevator.
Fur becomes wrapped
as a second skin,
licks my petals like a lover.

As I move my
feet touch and lead me to a place
where the only sound is the rush
of an underground waterfall,
the only sight is the
most moonless black,
the only smells are ghosts of
bear grease,
rock, and fear,
with the singular
and unquenchable craving
for fire.

Popping Tar Bubbles

At high noon, in mid-July,
countless tar bubbles
on every street corner,
   sealing edges of sewers,
   full of heat and water,
   softness and pressure.

In the raw ways of summer,
they would break in our hands
like the moments of exposure
inside boxy cameras,
the ones I keep finding
film spools for
the next thirty years;
Brownies, Roy Rogers,
and twin-lens Rolleiflex.

In a photo
the colors are four;
gray the street,
black the tar,
clear,
the water on my fingers,
white,
the sun, the sundress,
and the corners of boys' eyes.

We had workers;
three blocks of kids.
We had material;
buckets of tar poured
by smelly city trucks
the year before.
And like farmers,
   the ones far away

who grew food that appeared
mysteriously at our stores,
we had faith.

We prayed for rain and
  a day of coloring books indoors,
then prayed for
days of steady sun,
to swell the bubbles full,
thin, and round...
for a rampant harvest,
tan lines on our backs,
and a dozen close calls
with Buicks.

The Man Who Taught Me to Swim

My stepfather seemed
happiest in a swimsuit,
shedding gabardine
that hovered around him
like a tattersall phantom
at his civil service job.
Home movies showed his toothy grin
grow wider,
the less he had on,
and the closer he was to water.

In the 20's,
he swam whole Sundays
with Johnny Weissmueller
at Rainbow Beach,
the beach that curves
like a seashell
in the palm of South Shore,
the beach, a mother to orphans.
Stepdad was a Johnny, too,
and while one went on to Tarzan,
the other raised two brothers
on a diet of depression spaghetti*,
sorted a collection of landlocked ties
along the closet door,
rays of a prism from light to dark,
and swam three strokes on our vacations
to find himself
already on the other side
of the motel pool.

*depression spaghetti: my stepfather's recipe of cooked spaghetti
topped with a #10 can of room-temperature tomatoes.

Darkroom

Massive in this small room,
the photography teacher
with his shock of blond hair,
a cold fire under the safety lamp,
speaks of solutions before us.

Different from your spareness,
warm, excitable,
always revealing what's hidden
in broad daylight,
outside these walls,
somewhere as distant as San Antonio--
where I see sun-rich skin
contrast with acres of tumblebrush
a hundred shades of beige.

This veiled room gathers thin leaves
close in black and white,
a shadowed voice lectures me
as colors collide on a bleached wall,
the months you are gone.

I lift a photo wet from a pan, you
in front of your friend's linocuts,
that wise old mentor.
His eyes young with energy,
severity of the ancients in yours.

A negative for months in a drawer.
Now Chicago is all November,
in the dark I wake, I go home
in the dark,
hands move in dark liquids
in the lab, by an open window,
I hang your photo from a clothespin,
to dry, become brilliant,
as the Texas of your youth,
as the summer of my future.

Shabbona Park District Swimming Pool

You can feel the warmth
from hot water pipes,
   as you lean against the wall
   to pull up your swimsuit.
Locker doors, pink as grapefruits,
   wriggle like freshly-caught salmon.
I imagine painting high on the ceiling -
   glossy souvenir plates
   from Florida,
   oversized seashells,
   faceless and exotic,
revealing thin ribbons of flesh like
lingerie straps of a woman,
   as she runs for a bus.

I change,
to a world of rubber, cold water
and chlorine,
where I've vowed to carve my body
   with wet breath
   and a thousand gestures of arms,
breast, back, kick, crawl.
Tons of cares dip beneath me,
at the same time reject me,
keeping me afloat,
like some branch fallen in a river.

Chicago's January,
my lungs gasp
a reminder of my birth,
in mud and bark and snow,
so unlike Chief Shabbona himself,
   old, wise,
who swam tirelessly,
in rivers twice as old, nearby.

I see him rise, wet,
   into the forest,
returning with a deer dragged
on a travois.
They move together
   through deep white crystals,
   back to his people's camp.
And now, whatever I've gathered
   from these waters,
   I can only take back
to the showers,
hissing like radiators,
catching my body
in the mirror
on my way
to my quilt-covered
   bed,
where an indian waits
   in a book
   that I read.

The Building That Does Not Dance

> "...pushing up to crowd and be crowded, to
> grind against each other with a blind force
> moved by common greed."
>
> *Frank Lloyd Wright*

Sears Tower is where the sun rises and sets
on hundreds of glass windows,
on thousands of yesterday's transactions,
and at night,
the moon passes silently
through its phases overhead,
while the building,
calculated to be changeless,
is positioned like a missile
below the New Mexican desert.

This tower,
a giant dancer
that does not dance,
is a frozen steel chorus line,
that only thaws through the camera's eye,
where angles at war
move and melt
to the cold stare of film.
For one-hundred-and-three floors,
photocopiers go off like flashbulbs,
their blips of light
gathered by wide-angle lenses.
White chalk buildings
on Adams Street,
rub light on the tower
like strobes that fill in
cracks and flaws with a
neutral radiance.
Branches of the Chicago River
splash edges of film,
and Wacker Drive,
where cars drive close,
is pulled tightly on a sprocket.

The photos eventually end up in Spain,
while tower executives on the
sixty-third floor imagine
shoppers with hoppers of Lladro figurines
from the Sears in Madrid,
while the telephoto lens puts Sears Tower
in that most heightened sensibility -
devoid of people.
The building sways even without wind,
but the shutter stops it dead.
Odd two-by-fours,
this armload of projections
could well be poking through clouds
in West Germany... Japan...
but the caption reads Chicago, Illinois.
The town billions will never visit,
and millions catch second-hand
     through photographs.

Quote from the Canon AE-1 instruction manual:
"If you photograph a building from street level,
the upper part of the building will look smaller
and appear to lean backwards."
The building that does not dance,
dances on for the camera,
while those in charge
of the silos in New Mexico
hold inquiring eyes at a distance,
hoping to keep shutter curtains drawn
as well as they veil
bombs underground,
and across their known affairs with violence,
letting only enough light leak through
to silhouette the force of power
and the spectacles built in its honor.

Confusing reports on the arms race:
We see photos of hundreds of demonstrators,
while not a single bomb.
The people, very much alive,
not dead,
as if bombs,
with every report of deployment,
were fertility symbols,
opening doors of highrises,
filling streets with
    breathing, intelligent fruit,
filling newspapers
with crowded photographs.
Would dropping a bomb or two
    really make a dent
    in our incredible numbers?

Billions look out
toward a cold, passive eye
of some viewfinder in the sky.
Sears Tower.
The tallest building in the world.
Photographs in magazines
and in your kids' school books,
show how sleek it is,
how tall and sexy.
Repeating images of glass
    from other buildings
perform a dizzy dance
of replication.
A building for every book,
A bomb for every breadbasket.

Self-Portrait in a Game of Pool

Chalky fingers.
Lean as a cue stick.
Hair slicked and severe
    as an eight ball.

The clap of billiard balls
summons up a smoky atmosphere
that pulls clouds away
    from my sharpened eyes.

Students in checkerboard shorts,
    monogrammed shirts,
rely only on colors in solids and stripes
to transform pool into
the fast food of games.

Pool is no game, but needs
    an inborn posture,
thriving on triangular rays
    from overhanging lamps,
vague hues, violets and
    soft greys - loaded with smoke.
Floor echos from a random shuffle
    of shoes.
The table accepts no nonsense.

    There is the waiting,
        the systematic stalking
around and around the table,
the lean of the body, the arrangement
        of limbs,
the curled and grasping hand poses,
a knowledge of angles, padded
        bumpers,
        calculated decisions,
        soft strokes.

The Squash Garden
Eighteen Haikus

A wave at high tide
sun floods through the squash garden
night brings a sand bed.

Cross pollination,
last year's drought, a one night's stand,
stolen fluids, no fruit.

The landlord's muddy yard,
seed in April, twelve-foot August,
each blossom a wink.

Like sets of new sheets,
fresh topsoil covers the bed,
where squash will cry out.

Rippled, open, awed,
watch the squash blossom make love,
close her legs at night.

Cups of rain water
spill through lips of blossoms,
wash summer passion.

Petals wither now
squash blossoms freshly ravished,
sexy gourds balloon. .

Squash lie under tents,
leaves garish as old fabric,
each shadow a song.

Vines curl and grip to
parking lot and lettuce leaves,
pull squash toward the fall.

Stalks hold fast to squash
ovens hotly try to pierce,
steaming table gold.

Butter and honey
bathe squash in a lover's balm,
make forks look wealthy.

Squash, a side issue,
till their long butternut boats
made dock in my garden.

Hues tumbles like leaves,
we collect squash in wide bowls,
most never sample.

Water, steam, soft pith,
the squash changes for our sake,
warms our teeth, blood, skin.

Squash, stimulant fruit,
a fertile seed of nightbeds,
sleep with temptation.

My man moans, talks hot,
squash winter in root cellar,
gardener gets her love.

Night limbs weave and doze,
vines reach for the moon and back,
our desires compost.

Mornings, I count seeds,
measure lengths of ground for spring,
dream of fiery squash.

Dream Before the Earthquake

Alone in a room
of my mother's house,
packing her clothes for a
    long journey,
pulling family pictures from the wall,
where a long, deep crack reappears,
    there when we first
    moved in, covered for years
with the wealth from my mother's loom,
that wove the rebozos she danced in.

Far away now
I open drawers of my mother's things,
from top to bottom,
I descend
each tier as if it were a tall building,
    each drawer full of rubble, dust, and sand,
the bottom drawer drops into my hands
    like a baby full of answers,
quietly I lift out
    a dozen cut roses,
while in the corner
the black lace of a fan.

El Dia de los Muertos/All Soul's Day

A pot of chocolate melts and
   bubbles like mud,
fresh, sweet corn
releases starch
in a room scrubbed
for El Dia de los Muertos,
   cooked food
smells wildly of life,
     while paper-mache skulls
     look humble, clean, and
angry in their sleep,
shaped for our own
future death.

This afternoon,
a little boy from the Segundo barrio
   bites into a rock candy skull
   bearing his own name,
his soft cheekbones point
at the autumn sun
behind him,
his eyes narrow on his twin sister,
   where she stands frozen
   to the earth,
dangling a doll.

The night sky is
full of stars,
tips of skeletons' fingers
pressing against dark glass.
All the dead lean toward us,
and trace the outline
of our scissors on folded paper.
   Old family stories,
   legends how some have died,
make a map on the Mexican heart,
with roads wide and brilliant this night,
by dawn, have zig-zagged
in our sight.

The Invisible

Would you like to become invisible?
Observe the party circus, penetrate
   the highly guarded, regarded
     society,
peek into ledgers of corporate business,
as if no one were watching?
Then become the maid, the waitress, the
   underling, the one who wanders the room
   with a tray of cocktails and hors d'oeuvres.
and listen, listen,
in this invisible, sightless
   mist you finally can listen,
   to the bald viciousness,
   the diamond-throated agendas,
   ringing like empty glasses.

What is it like to be among the "disappeared"?
Then be a Central American peasant,
work for a dollar a day,
eat every tortilla accompanied by
   some modest salt,
while your skin burns slow
   and deep to coffee.
At sunset, look over the acres
   you have harvested,
and feel how the harvest
is pulled far away
from your family's mouths
to another country,
where other hands,
much like your own,
grasp a tray of cocktails
   and hors d'oeuvres.

And how is it that without land,
without harvests,
   you start acting as if
   you weren't invisible,
as if the cloak of distances,
the fog of shrouded
   news reports on Central America
didn't exist,
as if your eyes were the only eyes
   that could really see,
your own country - long ago,
the way it was
in the very beginning.

On the Other Side

I guide the sleeve
through the sewing machine
and the running stitches
are like the steps that
   followed the map
   my brother made.

All the way into Texas,
the sun threw down relentless heat
   on all my babies,
   too little to travel at night.
Now the sewing lamp stares down
   ten hours
on the veins of my hands,
that swell like rivers to be crossed.

We groped for hours for dry land,
now material pulls through hands
   like rough rock by Friday,
from one day to the next I cross,
my fingertips form the cruxifix
at sunrise
to make it to my stairs
by night.

The Last Father

I count bags of grain every night
like I count my children
before they go off to sleep.
One missing,
and the thick-faced soldiers
with lifeless eyes call me "traitor",
collaborator with the guerillas.
Not enough of the
government-issue grain
in my larder,
and I've been "feeding the enemy",
not enough heads to count
in my kitchen,
and I've been giving my children
   to fight in the mountains.
My mother told me
   she can't remember a time
   when there was peace,
even when corn in the fields
bloomed more yellow
than the sun.
And the priest told me
   there's only
   "three generations left
   to turn things around",
Or there will be no more
   El Salvador.
A year ago my husband
   disappeared in the jungle
   to the sound of snapping limbs,
and that day last month
   my eldest son climbed and
   blended into the mountains
like a new leaf uncurling
among others on a strong vine,

our house was filled with
moans of labor pains,
moans as many as grains
that fill a sack,
which would not breathe
a word of our transition.
My eldest daughter gave birth
just before the soldiers
made their periodic check,
and could not tell
from his small, wise face,
they were staring
into all our futures.

**Man Learned to Dance
Before He Could Walk**

Under ancient skies,
as soon as mankind
had a sense of free will
and could walk away
from an emotional situation,
he usually did.

Hoeing with bare hands,
spots and stripes of
    wild animals
    ever before your eyes,
when freedom was traveling
    as far as your legs
    could carry you,
the few who ventured out were
    considered fools.
Freedom only served you
    a few years, anyway,
running, walking, climbing,
    but never dancing,
dancing took your whole heart,
dancing was essentially supernatural.
When crops were dried and
    your stomach small and
    nasty-tempered,
a rain dance was serious business,
    hope of the last resort,
    the final embrace before
another cycle began.
Who dances on graves?
Who dances for joy?
but only those released
from pain,
who did not walk away,
but persevered,

came out dancing.
When spirits need to be summoned
or the Lord God worshipped -
   man, with all his
   strength, danced.
One day was allotted for your birth,
another for death,
and a handful for celebration
   and dancing.
The rest of the days
were vines of a bean plant
curling higher and higher
towards heaven.
Festive costumes, food,
   brought together by
   El Shaddai,
to be enjoyed by proxy,
in places higher
   than those created
   from corn, or dust.
To celebrate was an honor,
   a piece of eternity
    granted according to calendar
   or elders.
What more was man than
   beans, grain
   and a burning center,
illuminated fully when he danced,
exposed to the community
   he dare never walk away from.
Returning to his fields,
   to the brushes with animals,
   he stayed close to the fire at night,
the pagentry of dancing hovered like memories
   around drops of sweat,

for months humming low, but steady
    like a flame,
shrouding even the most simple lives
    in mystery.
But tonight, in the city,
you ask me to go out dancing,
there is no harvest, nor has
    my sister married, and the snow
    has continued to fall for
    two weeks.
Is bad news on your lips?
The kind we can scatter like dust
under our feet
and crush in passionate whirls?
I walk past bakeries
with new cheesecakes in
    windows,
mirrors from above and below
    slice light
    across your eyes and make you dizzy,
the sidewalk angle makes you
want to tumble in,
buy a cake with nobody in mind,
this heart searching for
    a celebration of one,
        with no one to dance with.

Lucifer, The Morning Star

the nine jewels you wore,
despite their brilliance,
detected every flaw.

the beauty that turned violent,
the wisdom - corrupted.

you, who beat fierce white wings
    to rise above the
    fiery stones of God
    where you kept watch,

stoked the fire placed inside, how by surprise,
it rushed out, likewise consumed you,
making everything in your path a desert,
you, a man expelled, even
    from your own graveyard.

cast from heaven
    to earth,
in spite of your arguments, the hand
    grasping Michael's elbow,
    the pointed finger of your rights,
your desire now, to deaden
everything with breath,
    even from the womb.

the one who made you like
    coal into a diamond,
tossed you away when your
    own coldness broke you,
double-faced, like a cloven hoof.
the one who wove your perfect skin
    on a loom,
    with threads of

eternal tension,
came down to earth,
letting others tear at his,
his back,
plaited like a crude basket,
meant only for a season of
transporting fish to market,
his face and shoulders,
    glistening with medallions of blood,
    dripping into complicated rivers,
as they dried in the
Golgotha sun.

    Ah this tooth, this bone
of the people,
polished white
in candle-power of the resurrection,
to pay the price
of exquisite gems you hocked
    in every pawnshop of desire
    as you whisper,
"Yes, see my jeweled complexion,
see, how it reflects,
    how beautiful you are."

Paris Windows

They can see out, but you
   can't see in,
the smooth French clay
   of the building, like a
   facial, like a
mask,
cracks slightly under the
   lamp of the sun,
fine lines lead to crowsfeet,
where they gather tightly
   around corners
   of windows,
keeping pigeons company.

Brashness and heat seem to
   radiate from inside a
   bedroom.
Sheets pulled down,
the bed empty,
   you can still hear the
   argument of last night,
followed by hours of embraces,
long strokes of hands
over hips and faces.

The red paper window shade
   blows out
   over the street,
like one of those cellophane noisemakers
   at New Year's
   that tensely unwinds,
tickles you on the nape of the neck,
then retreats quickly,
   out of sight,
leaving the air still
   as a Japanese shrine.

The couple is now at work.
A steak thaws on the counter,
a little blood mixes with ice,
and melts into a silken thread
down the throat of the drain.
The family poodle tugs
　　the cord of the window shade,
　　with his teeth,
　　in the dark.

The Wheel

I.

Take this Incan prophecy for a spin,
"The wheel will eventually
    ruin the world."
And using granite, fine grains of wood,
metal, and rubber,
the world's wheel makers
drove fiercely to ignore this advice,
leaving history in a cloud of dust.

Even the simple Amish,
whose animals worked lands
criss-cross with roads that stretch
as far as a buggy can roll,
past cornfields, wheatfields,
highway cloverleaves,
into the hub of town,
have found the spirit of this place
as one only a wheel
or a covetous thought
can touch.
The Amish say,
better we meekly use the wheel on route
to church, to stop for supplies,
to deliver our dead,
and quickly return to our hens and lambs,
than yearn to see
all the actions of the world
in rotation.

II.

If a tunnel were dug
straight as an axle
through the world's spokes,
it would culminate on a cliff,

a Peruvian village
encircling a stone calendar.
Wheel-shaped, wide as three men,
hand-deep in symbols,
as rugged as the Andean footpaths.
How did it get up here,
on paths too narrow and steep
to be traced by any wheel.
"Wheels should serve God,
    not man," say the priests.
And on the other side of the world,
Tibetan monks look up
to the Himalayas.
It's a feast day,
and smiling children rise
on bright red ferris wheels
made from wood and turned
by the elders' hands.
Saffron monks sit cross-legged
turning prayer wheels,
putting revolutions of truth
into motion,
without cart or chariot,
skeining prayers up
past the wheel-shaped sky.

III.

Train tracks no longer useful
connect stolen lands.
Tribal ears of America
against the ground,
wringing a bloody history
of trails of tears,
stage coaches,
covered wagons,

broken wheels
that claw the desert
like ribcages of dead steer.

Cities wound tight as wheels,
spring out of watches,
roll onto expressways
liquid with mirage,
thick with smog.
Age-old hillsides
now fluted with concrete,
find only tires, not man,
touch the ground.
Cars roll out of garages,
down wheel tributaries
that rock with earthquakes,
splash tidal waves of Porsches
up ramps into parking lots
    of tanning salons,
    gourmet cooky shops,
    urban western wear,
and headquarters of tire companies
50 stories high.

The Fourth Fiber

I.

When it comes to fables,
after flax, wool, and cotton,
silk has spun the wildest yarns,
and one of the longest,
    the 6000-mile Silk Road
connected end to end
by finest strands
    of raw silk
from the
never-empty
bobbin of China,
stretched and pulled
over rocky crags
of the Mediterranean shore.

They waited for the culture
    behind the cloth,
those Italians who
    brought huge pots
    of water to boil,
where plump cocoons
    drop,
    kill worms, and
    unwind fibers
into long, soft fingers
the shade of Medieval parchment.
As the water steamed and tumbled
    they waited,
    but the Chinese sent armies
    of silk merchants,
rich in fabrics,
poor in cultivation.
Never missing a chance to turn

irony into romance,
the Italians invented spaghetti instead.

II.

For awhile, like oil to Mexicans,
silk to the Chinese
    was a national treasure,
until a young princess,
foolish, in love,
subjected a coolie entourage
to every temperature
    and altitude of her whims
over Himalayas
to the door of her Indian prince.
After the wedding,
    he peeled layer
    after filmy layer
of silk from her body,
while she broke open
her headdress
with delicate, defiant hands,
    revealing silk worm eggs
    and seeds of the mulberry tree
    as her wedding gift to him.
That very night, she conceived,
    the first of the new legacy,
    children to weave silk
    into saris of woven wind.

Quarter American

The full moon hangs
   in a crowded sky,
a clean button,
crisply sewn and shiny
   in a closet of unpressed
   and worn garments,
buildings poke unwanted holes
   in black velvet,
as they pin glass and steel
to skyscape.

A half moon in Hamburg,
the crescent in Japan,
our pie charts grow thinner
at yet another table
surrounded in grey suits.

And now, for three days in New York,
I look at no one but
   waitresses, bus drivers,
   ticket takers, elevator operators,
like some relic on
a conveyor belt,
I pass on display
   in front of
   smearings, tangles,
   and stones with shapes
like wind and waterfalls
from a dozen vital
third world cultures
   that respond to me
   like the worn quarter I am,
   devalued by my aimless wanderings.

The Writing's on the Wall

Every morning,
a painter enters a room
longing for an even field
of color
as pastel and harmonious
as sleep.
He holds a brush,
heavy with paint,
and begins to work the bare walls.

A wall just painted is
a long, wide tongue
of geometry,
a desert of sandy beige, off-white,
    eggshell, crystal blue.
He paints one color at a time,
an intoxication of simplicity.
He kneels on a canvas dropcloth,
as if beginning a Japanese ceremony.
The lid released, he can feel
    the color already,
the mixing stick
beats the sides of the can
like a drum,
the oily fragrance hits his nostrils
as sharply as a lightswitch
fires the glaring bare bulb.
Just a few steps away,
sheer will consumes the walls,
covering a multitude of sins.
There's a vastness
above reach of our arms
where only with ladders
    is there access,
    to a section,
    to a shelf,
    to a book,
    to a word.

And Lead Him Not Into Penn Station

Were you headed for Italy, or Florida?
You can't remember now
as you sit in this "Ironbound" park,
five minutes from Newark International,
the place your body fled
in the biggest airplane
that could get off the ground
fifteen years ago.

You shook off your old, dark nature
like a black leather jacket,
like a New Jersey toxic cloud,
to wander the neighborhood in your absense.
It was given respect as a memory,
treated like one of their dead.

"A prophet is never honored in his own country"...
and as you charted a map of your own design,
analyzed a culture that clings together
with the promise of adventure,
you saw a country that stretched highways
beyond these root-cramped parks
and dimly-lit blocks of your neighbors.
You told them the seamless dream of the outside.
They warned you it was too vast,
would encourage and humor your rootlessness,
yet require endless production,
sun, perpetual watering,
then turn you down flatly
to return to your natural habitat.

Now as you come back these odd weekends,
poke your head into bars
whose owners used to watch you read
Mao's little red book for hours in Portuguese,

you find they don't ask why you were gone,
why you're here again.
You pause by your bench in Independence Park,
to see if your initials
have been worn by broad backs
of the new regulars,
factory workers you struggled
never to become.

Instead you combed the beaches for shells
for awhile, but the shoreline
stretched too long, as did the days,
and when you taught those black kids in DC,
you made sure it was summer school
   or as a substitute,
a way they couldn't keep
your back to the board.
And now at that long-distance company
at midnight, the hour of
the third shift back home,
you reach any part of the world
in a few touches,
but the dial tone makes you form fists,
sounding like the hum from the plant
where your father worked.

Those nights in your folks' flat,
insomnia fills corners
of your old room,
surging with Coltrane,
the walls, lined in maps
of places you've longed to be,
but haven't found the chance,
and your old bureau,
full of your mother's linens,

makes your room like a room you enter
where you haven't yet turned on the light
and a soft voice scares you.

The night is full of a thousand dark insects,
whose single songs, like yours,
get obscured by numbers,
and like them, too, you hover
by the pink charges of worn neon
that appears every three blocks.
And as you move through the streets,
it's at these places you sit down again,
pull the pad from your backpocket,
get busy, make plans, draw routes,
think things through, imagine
your next move.

And soon, hundreds of miles away,
your key unlocks a room
of other people's furniture.
D.C.
hot, white, and the stark world
you escape to,
that pretends to embrace
all regions, all peoples,
but empties like a sprung cage at night.
You say to yourself,
look, I am not where I was before,
I am not like my friends on assembly lines,
who cling, like shopkeepers' awnings,
to Ferry Street.
You walk up and down Ferry Street
with that one-eyed Spaniard who pirated your boyhood,
you ailing father.
And trying to fall asleep,

you fall under wet concrete,
where initials press into hardness
from a stick,
you startle, get up,
sit and stare at your hands,
you stand, move your feet,
but they keep taking you to
airports, train stations,
tickets appear between your fingers
from nowhere.

Black & White: A Zebra's View

They say I look so
much like a horse,
but historically,
the horse looks like me,
though more thick and plain,
he is occasionally dappled,
yet without a real flourish on him.
His hooves are earthbound,
rooted to the soil, galloping,
huge legs beat prairies
into clouds that dirty his back.
Yoked to a plow, he's forced
to push slowly over clods
and boulders in the fields.
Everywhere he goes, his looks
are imported,
a refugee from OPEC nations.

On the other hand,
without training, wagers, or odds,
my close-cropped fur fits tight
as a lycra swimsuit,
I streak like the Sunday paper
off the presses,
and all you can make out
is my backside
as I quickly race away.
My Olympic leaps break records
over brush,
narrow streams, and crags,
never stumbling,
I raise dust tornados
around my hooves
and rise completely
off the ground.

Some say, even in death
our kind goes for the dramatic.
Only the lion can overtake us,
or the rare warrior,
who fling our coats
toward the acacia trees,
in ribbons of day, ribbons of night.

Jeronimo

Cynthia Gallaher, a native Chicagoan, has published poetry in small press magazines and anthologies around the country for the last fifteen years, most recently seen in *Emergency Tacos* anthology. She won the Poetry Prize in *Korone*'s Anthology of Illinois Women Writers, and recently was awarded a Community Arts Grant from the Chicago Office of Fine Arts. She is active with Illinois Coalition for Safe Food, and other environmental groups. This is her first book of poetry. She is currently working on a poetry manuscript dealing with the subject of animals, entitled, *Other Species.*